This book belongs to:

_____

this book is dedicated to my little ladies

Harper, Piper & Juniper

May you always feel connected to the wisdom
of your mind, body and spirit.

An Able Alchemy Book
Glen Ellyn, IL 60137

The Rainbow In Me, Text, Illustration and Photography © 2025 by Able Alchemy LLC.

All rights reserved. No part of this book may be reproduced, transmitted, or stored in an information retrieval system in any form or by any means, graphic, electronic, or mechanical, including photocopying, taping, and recording, without prior written permission from the publisher.

Library of Congress Number: 2025921226

First Edition, 2025
Book design by Courtney O'Keeffe. Illustrations were created in Procreate over the photography captured by Sarah Crost. To learn more about Sarah and her work, visit www.sarahcrost.com.

To learn more about Courtney and her work at Able Alchemy, visit www.ablealchemy.com.

ISBN 979-8-9932812-0-9

The Rainbow in me

A Journey Through the Chakras

Written & Illustrated by
Courtney O'Keeffe

Photography by
Sarah Crost

able alchemy

There is a **rainbow** inside my body, with colors I can feel.

Each color has a message, and spins just like a wheel.

Let's take a journey together, from the bottom to the top.

Let's explore the **rainbow**, that twirls and never stops!

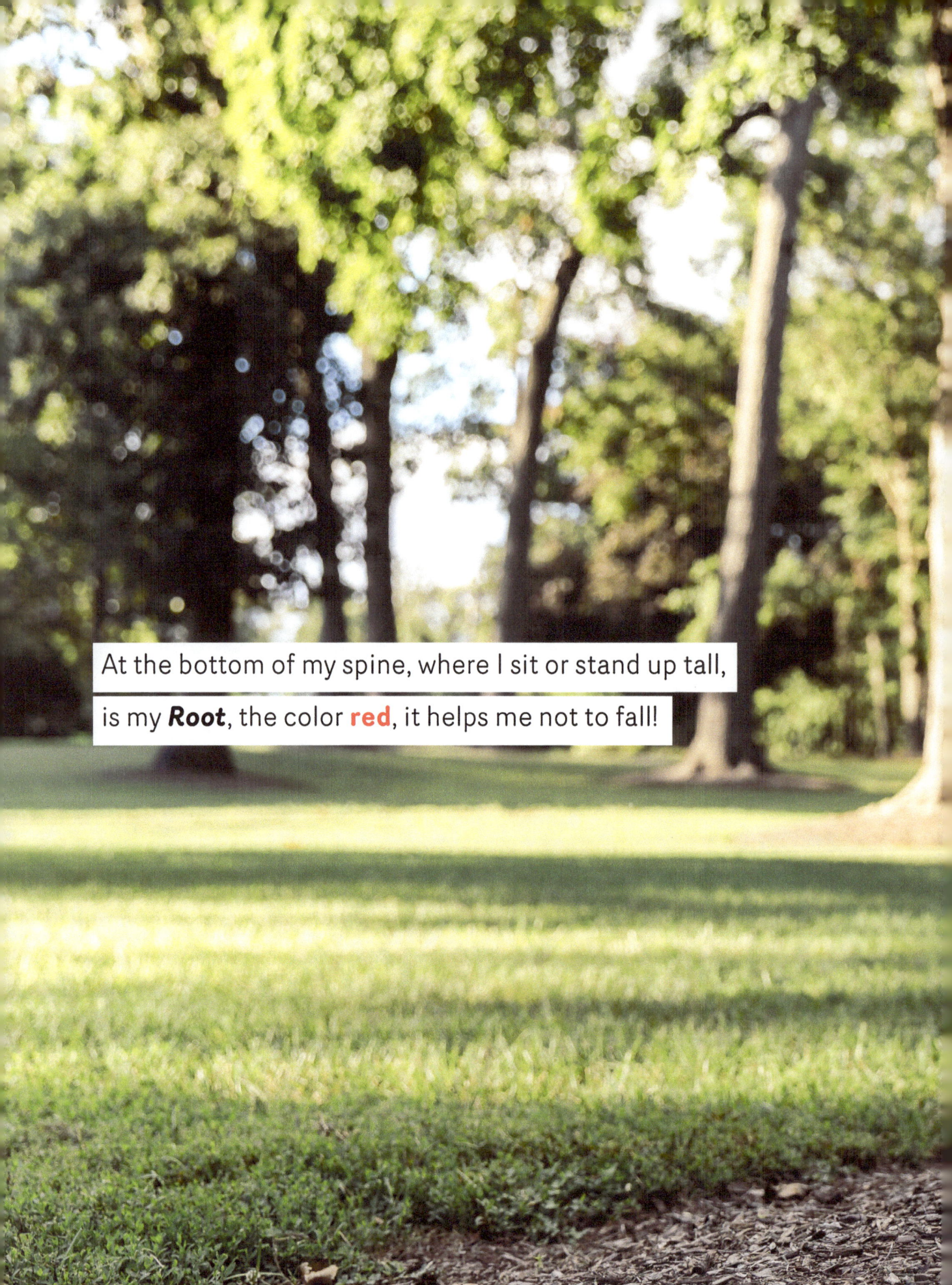

At the bottom of my spine, where I sit or stand up tall,
is my **Root**, the color red, it helps me not to fall!

When I hug my parents, I know I'm not alone.

When I'm cozy in my bed, I feel safe like a sturdy stone.

When I run in the grass, I feel stable like a tree.

Connected to the Earth, that's the **red** in me.

Just below my belly, where my feelings like to stay, is my **Sacral**, bright orange, guiding me each day.

When I draw a picture, I'm creative like an artist.

When I fall off my bike, I feel sad. I tried my hardest.

When I go somewhere new, I'm filled with curiosity.

Embracing my emotions, that's the **orange** in me.

Above my belly button, there's something powerful and bright, it's my **Solar Plexus**, burning yellow, it gives me all my might!

When I perform for an audience, I'm a wonder to behold.

When I try something on my own, I'm confident and bold.

When I eat healthy foods, I charge my inner battery.

Knowing I am worthy, that's the yellow in me.

In the middle of my chest, there's a space for love to grow,
the **Heart**, gleaming green, where kindness goes to flow.

When I make new friends, I am loyal and I am true.

When I apologize for a mistake, I see another point of view.

When I help clean up the park, I support my community.

Showing compassion and empathy, that's the **green** in me.

On my neck, where my voice can sing and speak out loud, is my **Throat**, colored blue, it helps me stand out in the crowd.

When I tell a story, it's like a book right off the shelf.

When I share my dreams, I believe in my future self.

When I speak up for others, I help all voices be free.

Sharing my truth with the world, that's the blue in me.

Just above my eyebrows, where my thoughts dance in my head, is my **Third Eye**, glowing indigo, where imagination spreads.

When I have a new idea, I share the visions that I see.

When I sit and think about what to do, I know I have the key.

When I listen to my inner voice, there's always possibility.

Trusting my own intuition, that's the **indigo** in me.

At the tippy-top of my head, the part that looks up to the sky, is my **Crown**, shining *violet*, it makes me feel like I can fly!

When I feel something I can't see, I connect to something greater.

When I experience magic, it's a gift from our creator.

When I embrace the mystery of life, I live happily.

Believing in a higher power, that's the **violet** in me.

Let's close our eyes and feel, from our **Root** up to our **Crown**.

The rainbow lives inside us, and wants to spin around.

Let's take a deep breath together, slowly in and out.

Your rainbow lives inside you, of that, there is no doubt.

ROOT (red)

When do you feel safe and strong?

What helps you feel grounded when you're upset?

SACRAL (orange)

What are some feelings you had today?

What's your favorite way to be creative?

SOLAR PLEXUS (yellow)

When do you feel proud of yourself?

What's something brave you've done lately?

HEART (green)

What's one kind thing you did this week?

How do you show someone you care?

THROAT (blue)

What's something you love to talk about?

When have you spoken up for yourself or a friend?

THIRD EYE (indigo)

Have you had a big idea lately? What was it?

Can you think of a time you listened to your "inner voice"?

CROWN (violet)

What makes you feel connected to something bigger than you?

When have you felt peaceful or full of wonder?

Rainbow Affirmations

ROOT (red)
"I am safe."
"I belong."

SACRAL (orange)
"I am creative."
"It is okay to feel my feelings."

SOLAR PLEXUS (yellow)
"I am strong."
"I can do hard things."

HEART (green)
"I am kind."
"I am loved, and I love others."

THROAT (blue)
"My voice matters."
"I love sharing my ideas."

THIRD EYE (indigo)
"I trust myself."
"I can imagine anything."

CROWN (violet)
"I am connected to something bigger."
"I am full of wonder."

Chakra Cheat Sheet for Parents

A quick guide to understanding your child's energy centers

ROOT (red)

Safety, stability, connection to home and Earth
Grounding activities: walking barefoot, hugs, routines

SACRAL (orange)

Emotions, creativity, pleasure, change
Support with: art time, emotional check-ins, dancing

SOLAR PLEXUS (yellow)

Confidence, willpower, independence
Support with: encouraging choices, celebrating effort

HEART (green)

Love, empathy, forgiveness, relationships
Support with: modeling kindness, talking about feelings

THROAT (blue)

Self-expression, truth, communication
Support with: storytelling, active listening, affirming voice

THIRD EYE (indigo)

Imagination, intuition, inner knowing
Support with: quiet time, visualization, dream-sharing

CROWN (violet)

Spiritual connection, wonder, big-picture thinking
Support with: nature, gratitude, asking open-ended questions